Picture Credits
t=top, tr=top right, tl=top left, bl= bottom left, br=bottom right, b=bottom, m=middle, ml=middle
left, mr=middle right

P9: Victor9876 (tr); P9: Chester Harding (ml); P12: Bobak Ha'Eri (mr); P13: Greg Hume (ml); P13:
0r14nd0 (b); P15: C.C.A. Christensen (tr), (mr); P16: Sean Kennelly (br); P17: Oscar Halling (tl); P17:
Gustave Dore (mr); P17: Harry Clarke (bl); P21: Wendy Keveney (ml); P25: Alkivar (ml); P26: David
Shankbone (br); P27: Kilnburn (tr); P27: Lee Paxton (b); P28: Ad Meskens (ml); P30: Cd637 (ml);
P30: The White Pelican (ml); P31: Kris Mast (m); P31: J. Robert Iko (b); P33: Lear 21 (bl); P37: Jan
Kronsell (ml); P37: Thomas R Machnitzki (mr); P37: H. Michael Miley (bl); P41: Quadzilla99adzil-
la99 (tl); P41: marine 69-71 (ml); P41: steve lipofsky (mr), (mr); P41: jimcchou (br); P43: transplanted
mountaineer (ml)

PAB-0912-0155

ISBN: 978-1-4867-1397-4

Fact Checker:
Jay Johnson

Written by
Sean Kennelly
Dan Carpenter

TABLE OF CONTENTS

D.Y.K.A.

DO YOU KNOW ABOUT...

How much do you know about famous Americans? Find awesome facts throughout the book as you learn more about some of the amazing Americans who shaped our nation. Just look for the D.Y.K.A. symbol!

GEORGE WASHINGTON
(1732-1799)
FATHER OF HIS COUNTRY

For eight long years during the American Revolution, George Washington was the commanding general of the Colonial Army. When the war finally ended in 1783, he just wanted to get back to farming on his lovely Mount Vernon estate. He wouldn't get to stay there long. Six years after the war ended, Washington reluctantly agreed to become the nation's first president. No one ran against him in that election because the nation understood that Washington was the right man for the job. After serving his first four years, he had to be talked into serving a second **term**. When aides suggested he serve a third term, he flatly refused. Even so, Washington was a superb president because he was a great man. He created a tradition that American presidents must be strong, admirable leaders who could be followed by the people.

George Washington was known as a man who said very little. For example, as president of the four-month long Constitutional Convention in 1787, he only spoke one time during floor debate. He did, however, write a lot of letters. In fact, 19,000 of them still exist. People realized that Washington was a history maker, so they held on to things he wrote. Sadly, his wife, Martha, burned all but three of the letters she and George wrote to each other. She did this to protect their privacy. Though he said little, he certainly looked like a president. Standing six feet and two inches tall, he towered above most other men. A man who knew Washington said that if 10,000 people were in a room, you would pick Washington as the president.

When his time as president ended in 1797, Washington returned home to tend to the farming he loved so much. Sadly, he would not do so for long. On a cold winter day in 1799, he got caught in the rain while checking his crops. Feeling sick, he came home and went to bed with a sore throat. Modern medicines make such illnesses harmless, but in the 1700s things were different. Washington died just two days later. He was only sixty-seven years old.

D.Y.K.A.

HIPPO TEETH!

By the time he became president, Washington only had one tooth left. However, he wore state-of-the-art hippopotamus tusk teeth, made especially for him with room for his one tooth to fit through.

Thomas Jefferson
(1743-1826)
The Great Statesman

Jefferson lived a fascinating life. He was **governor** of Virginia during the American Revolution, he was the third president, and he founded one of the nation's finest schools, the University of Virginia. But for Jefferson, perhaps his proudest moment was when, at age thirty-three, he wrote the Declaration of Independence. This was a handwritten letter to the British king, informing him that the thirteen colonies would no longer accept him as their leader. The Declaration is powerfully written, and its eloquent words will echo through time: "We hold these truths to be self-evident, that all men are created equal, that they are endowed by their Creator with certain **unalienable** rights, that among these are life, liberty, and the pursuit of happiness…"

Jefferson loved to learn and to read books. He once said, "I cannot live without books." His personal collection of books was the biggest in America. When he died, those books became the beginning of the Library of Congress, which today has over thirty-eight million books and is the largest library in the world. Jefferson's love of learning continued through his excitement over the Louisiana Purchase. He especially delighted in all the information and samples the explorers brought back from the new land.

His love for learning also included training future military leaders. On George Washington's advice, Jefferson convinced **Congress** to fund the Academy at West Point in New York in 1802. Later, Jefferson continued his quest to educate Americans when he founded the University of Virginia in 1819. The university is located near his home in Monticello, where he entertained students and professors alike until his death in 1826.

MERIWETHER LEWIS & WILLIAM CLARK
(1774-1809) • (1770-1838)
BROTHERS IN ADVENTURE

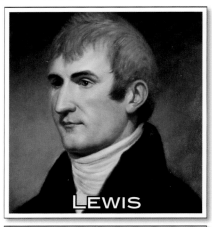

LEWIS

CLARK

When Meriwether Lewis was only five years old, his father died, and Thomas Jefferson took Lewis under his wing. He praised the boy for his "enterprise, boldness, and discretion." He saw in him a great sense of curiosity and adventure. Once he grew, Lewis joined the army on the frontier. There he learned Native American languages and customs. He also met William Clark. Clark came from a military family. His older brother, General George Rogers Clark, was a Revolutionary War hero. His family moved from Virginia to the Kentucky frontier where he fought against Native American tribes who were attacking settlers. Together, they fought side-by-side.

A few years later, Lewis was asked by President Thomas Jefferson to lead a group of explorers across the country to the Pacific Ocean. Jefferson wanted Lewis and his men to map the areas and bring back reports of the land, plants, animals, and the Native American tribes living there. Lewis knew he needed help leading the **expedition** and asked his old friend Clark to join him. Clark was very excited about the expedition!

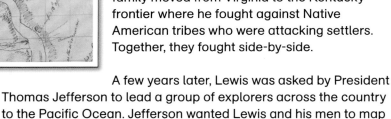

Together with about forty people (mostly hunters and soldiers called the Corps of Discovery), Lewis and Clark left St. Louis, Missouri, in May of 1804. They traveled thousands of miles across uncharted rivers, mountains, and prairies. Luckily, they had the help of a French-Canadian fur trader, Toussaint Charbonneau, and his teenage wife, Sacagawea. Sacagawea and her husband knew the territory well and led the men over the Rocky Mountains and down the Clearwater, Snake, and Columbia Rivers. Finally, after eighteen long months of exploring and mapping, they reached the Pacific Ocean. They stopped near the present-day city of Portland, Oregon, in November of 1805.

When they finally returned to St. Louis in September of 1806, they shared stories of the vast herds of buffalo and elk. They told of the rivers filled with beavers and the Native American tribes they encountered along the way. Most importantly, their maps became the first maps of the new territory. It showed future settlers and pioneers the way and inspired others to explore the vast land of America.

D.Y.K.A.

WILLIAM CLARK'S NICKNAME!
William Clark was nicknamed "Red Hair" by Native Americans. They had never seen a red-headed person before.

SACAGAWEA
(1788-1812)
GUIDING LIGHT IN THE WILDERNESS

It is believed that Native American **interpreter** Sacagawea was born around 1788. It is said she was the daughter of a Shoshone Indian chief, but she only lived among the Shoshone as a child. When she was twelve, an enemy tribe, the Hidatsa Indians, raided her camp, and she was taken captive. She was then sold to the trapper Toussaint Charbonneau, along with another girl known as "Otter Woman." The two became his wives and lived with him among the Hidatsa and Mandan Indians near what is now Bismarck, North Dakota, for four years.

Sacagawea was sixteen and pregnant with her first child when the Corps of Discovery, led by Lewis and Clark, arrived in the area. Lewis and Clark built a fort there where they spent the winter of 1804-05 and lived among the Mandan Indians. Charbonneau was hired as a Mandan interpreter for the expedition, but Lewis and Clark soon found that Sacagawea spoke the language better than her husband. So Sacagawea was asked to accompany her husband on the expedition. That winter, Sacagawea gave birth to her son, Jean Baptiste (who Clark nicknamed "Pompey" or "Pomp" for short).

That spring, Sacagawea, along with her husband, led the expedition through the western territories to the Pacific Ocean. Along the way, she acted as the primary interpreter and prevented attack on the expedition. How did she do this? Just by being there. Indian tribes knew that no one would bring a woman and child on a war party, so the expedition was viewed as a peaceful group.

After the expedition, Clark offered to pay for Sacagawea and her husband to relocate to St. Louis. He even offered to pay for Jean Baptiste's education, but Charbonneau refused and they returned to North Dakota. There, Sacagawea gave birth to a girl, Lizette, and later died at the age of twenty-four. Knowing how fond Clark was of the children, Charbonneau gave them to Clark and he raised them as his own. Their mother would be forever remembered for the role she played in the history of the United States.

D.Y.K.A.

SACAGAWEA'S NAME!

Sacagawea? Tsakakawias? Or Sacajawea? The spelling and meaning of Sacagawea's name has varied for years depending on who you ask. Her husband said her name meant bird woman which in the Hidatsa language would be spelled Tsakaka-wias. Many spell it with a "j" (Sacajawea) which is a Shoshone word for boat-launcher. Yet in Lewis and Clark's journals, it is mentioned seventeen times and spelled with a "g," so for most it is Sacagawea.

ANDREW JACKSON
(1767-1845)
"OLD HICKORY"

Andrew Jackson was born in 1767 on the border of North and South Carolina. When Andrew was fourteen, during the Revolutionary War, the British captured him and his sixteen-year-old brother, Robert. A redcoat officer struck each boy on the head with his sword. Andrew was left with a scar for life. His brother died of smallpox. A few months later, Andrew's mother died. Left alone with no family, young Andrew grew tough as he struggled to survive. In 1788, when he was twenty-one, he moved to the wild frontier town of Nashville, Tennessee. Nashville was an eight-year-old city where death by Indian attack was a real part of everyday life. Here, Jackson became a successful businessman and lawyer, and he entered state politics.

Andrew Jackson became a household name in America in 1815 when he won the Battle of New Orleans. This was the final battle of the War of 1812, and it was one of the most lopsided wins in history. About 2,042 British soldiers were killed or wounded, while only fifty-two American lives were lost. This smashing victory vaulted Jackson into national prominence, leading to his election as president fourteen years later.

Jackson was a very important president because he put politics into the hands of the average American. The six presidents before Jackson were **aristocrats**. Jackson was the first president from the frontier. He was a self-made man of the people. His tough background was evidenced by the fact that he carried two bullets inside him from gun battles. Jackson changed the nature of American politics, making it possible for everyone, regardless of wealth or family status, to play a role in the nation's government.

D.Y.K.A.

THE STOLEN ELECTION!

In 1824, Andrew Jackson ran for president for the first time, beating John Quincy Adams by 38,000 votes. He also had more **electoral votes** than Adams, beating him ninety-nine to eighty-four. However, the Constitution requires a candidate to have more than fifty percent of the electoral votes to win. So the **House of Representatives** awarded the presidency to Adams, son of the second president. Jackson was so angry that he began campaigning immediately for the next election, which he won.

ABRAHAM LINCOLN
(1809-1865)
THE GREAT EMANCIPATOR

Abraham Lincoln was born in a log cabin in Kentucky in 1809. Luckily, he was born to a mother who knew how to read and taught young Abe from the time he was a small boy. She also taught him to be honest and good to people. He was also tall. He grew to be six feet and four inches tall! This was one young man everyone had to look up to.

As he grew to manhood, Lincoln continued to borrow and read books. He eventually taught himself enough (by reading law books) to become a lawyer. He also decided to run for political office. Though he lost many times, he never gave up and eventually served in the state **legislature** and the US Congress. Later, he became president of the United States, even though he wasn't on the ballot of ten southern states.

Almost as soon as he took office, the Civil War broke out. It pained Lincoln to see his countrymen at war with each other. In his Gettysburg Address (given after the famous battle), he spoke not only of the ongoing war, but of his hope "that this nation, under God, shall have a new birth of freedom—and that government of the people, by the people, for the people, shall not perish from the earth."

Lincoln also issued the Emancipation Proclamation, finally bringing an end to slavery. Others were not happy with his decisions or the course of the war. Six days after the South surrendered, Lincoln was assassinated by John Wilkes Booth. The nation mourned, but Lincoln's words, works, and memory never left them.

D.Y.K.A.

LINCOLN'S HOUSE!

The actual cabin Lincoln was born in is gone, but a similar cabin from the same time period stands on his birthplace near Hodgenville, Kentucky. The 200-year-old cabin is preserved inside a beautiful marble building for all to see. However, the natural spring Lincoln's family drank from is still there, not far from the old cabin.

FREDERICK DOUGLASS
(1818-1895)
VOICE OF THE SLAVES

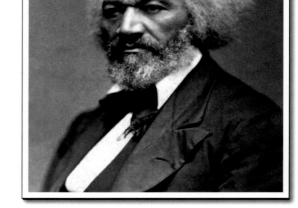

Frederick Douglass was born into slavery in Maryland in 1818. When he was twelve, his owner's wife taught him to read. This was highly unusual because most slave owners did not want their slaves to read. Slave owners feared that reading would open slaves up to ideas about freedom.

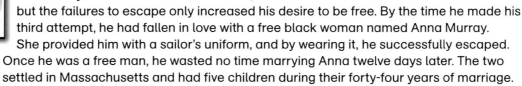

Douglass worked for various owners, but at age sixteen, he was rented out to a cruel master who whipped him nearly every day. Because of this brutal treatment, Douglass promised himself that he would escape within the year. He tried and failed twice, but the failures to escape only increased his desire to be free. By the time he made his third attempt, he had fallen in love with a free black woman named Anna Murray. She provided him with a sailor's uniform, and by wearing it, he successfully escaped. Once he was a free man, he wasted no time marrying Anna twelve days later. The two settled in Massachusetts and had five children during their forty-four years of marriage.

Three years after escaping, Douglass was asked to speak at an **abolitionist** meeting about his experiences as a slave. His speech was very powerful and painted a true, but horrible picture of slavery. He now began to speak regularly, and because he was such a gifted speaker, large audiences would always gather to hear him. His speeches were very important because they helped inform northerners of the terrors of slavery. This fed a growing northern anger over the use of slaves in the South, which eventually helped abolish slavery in America.

The issue of slavery divided Americans in the mid-1800s. Violent episodes such as **Bleeding Kansas** and **John Brown**'s raid on Harper's Ferry forced Americans to take sides. Eventually a four-year-long war, the Civil War, was fought to settle the issue. When the war was over, the practice of slavery was ended forever in America. Americans have Frederick Douglass to thank for helping make that a reality.

D.Y.K.A.

THE VOICE OF REASON!

Douglass was such an eloquent speaker that many people doubted he could have ever been enslaved. In order to prove he had indeed once been a slave, Douglass wrote his autobiography, *Narrative of the Life of Frederick Douglass*, in 1845. The terrors of slavery depicted in the book helped many Americans understand that a civilized nation could no longer allow slavery to take place within its boundaries.

Harriet Tubman
(1820-1913)
Freedom Fighter

Harriet Tubman was born Araminta "Minty" Ross to slave parents. As a child, she was taught to resist slave owners by her mother, Harriet. Her mother worked hard to keep their family together. When her owner came with a buyer for Tubman's younger brother, Tubman's mother threatened the owner and his buyer saying, "You are after my son; but the first man that comes into my house, I will split his head open." The bold move inspired Tubman, who escaped years later in 1849 in the middle of the night. Upon reaching the free state of Pennsylvania, Tubman wrote, "I looked at my hands to see if I was the same person now [that] I was free. There was such a glory over everything…and I felt like I was in Heaven."

Tubman took the name Harriet, honoring her mother. Her last name came from the free man she married, John Tubman. Though he was free, he was unwilling to help her escape, and she never returned to him. Tubman made a number of bold trips into slave territory to rescue the rest of her family and other slaves. She often made her trips during the winter, when people would be indoors and less likely to notice runaway slaves. She worked with other abolitionists, including Frederick Douglass, using the famous Underground Railroad—a series of safe homes and hiding places that helped the slaves to safely escape to the North. Of Tubman, Douglass said, "The midnight sky and the silent stars have been the witnesses of your devotion to freedom and of your heroism."

Tubman went on to serve as a nurse and a spy during the Civil War, knowing a victory by the North would result in freedom for the slaves. She even led an armed group of Union soldiers in a raid on some **plantations** in South Carolina that freed 700 slaves. When the war ended and all the slaves were freed, she continued to fight for equality. She also lent her voice to women's rights, working alongside Susan B. Anthony before Tubman's death in 1913. Her story continues to inspire people fighting for equality and civil rights.

HARRIET TUBMAN.

D.Y.K.A.

HARRIET TUBMAN'S BIRTHDAY!

Since she was born into slavery, the true age of Harriet Tubman was never known. Slave owners rarely kept birth records. Her death certificate lists her year of birth as 1815, while her gravestone is carved with the year 1820. Tubman herself had no real idea since she listed her birth year as 1820 on some documents and 1822 or 1825 on others.

ROBERT E. LEE
(1807-1870)
THE TACTICIAN

Robert E. Lee was born in Virginia in 1807 to a famous Revolutionary War general, "Light Horse Harry" Lee. Young Lee attended the US Military Academy at West Point and then served for thirty-two years in the US Army. When the Civil War began, Lee was the most respected officer in the army, so Lincoln offered Lee the top command position for the war. Lee declined the offer and then resigned from the army, saying he must remain true to his home state of Virginia. Confederate president Jefferson Davis quickly **commissioned** Lee into the Confederate Army, where he became one of its leading commanders, alongside General Joseph Johnston.

Robert E. Lee was probably the greatest American battle commander who ever lived. During the Civil War, Lee won battle after battle, though he was nearly always under-supplied and outnumbered. An example of this was at the Battle of Chancellorsville (1863), where Lee found his Rebel Army of 56,000 men facing a massive Union Army of 135,000 men. Amazingly, Lee not only won this battle, but he ran the Union Army off the battlefield, forcing them to flee across the Rappahannock River under the cover of darkness.

Lee was famous for dividing his army into two groups, even when heavily outnumbered. At the second Battle of Bull Run (1862), he sent half of his army all the way around to the rear of the Union forces. This caused the Union general to lose track of both parts of Lee's army, and of course, it led to yet another southern victory. Lee divided his army in a similar way in the Seven Days Battle (1862). This so confused the northern general that he reported Lee was using 200,000 troops, when he in fact had only 85,000.

Only late in the war, when northern advantages in numbers and supplies took their toll, did Lee find it impossible to continue to outwit Union generals. When the war finally ended, Lee's once proud Army of Northern Virginia was starving and out of ammunition, a shadow of its former self.

D.Y.K.A.

THE STOLEN MANSION!
Robert E. Lee lived in Arlington, Virginia, in the Custis-Lee Mansion, a home built by George Washington's adopted grandson. Just a month after the Civil War began, the Union army turned the mansion's yard into a cemetery, placing graves all the way up to the front porch. This was to make sure Lee could never return and occupy the beautiful home. Those graves became the beginning of Arlington National Cemetery, the nation's primary military graveyard.

Ulysses S. Grant
(1822-1885)
The Hero of Appomattox

When Ulysses S. Grant was born in Ohio in 1822, his parents named him Hiram Ulysses Grant. But he never liked the fact that his initials spelled HUG, and as he left home at eighteen to attend the United States Military Academy, he hoped to change his name. Oddly, he got the chance the moment he arrived on campus. The **congressman** who recommended him to the school had erroneously written Grant's name down as Ulysses S. Grant. When Grant saw the new name, he liked the change. For the rest of his life, his only middle name was S.

During the first three years of the Civil War, President Lincoln could not find a general who understood how to take the large and powerful Union Army into Virginia and win the war. During that period, Lincoln's Army of the Potomac lost battle after battle, as he went through eight commanding generals. Finally, in 1863, Lincoln realized the best general in his army was Ulysses S. Grant. Grant had won a series of amazing victories in Mississippi and Tennessee.

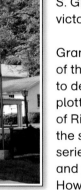

Grant was brought to Washington and put in charge of the Army of the Potomac. Lincoln ordered him to defeat Robert E. Lee and win the war. Grant plotted a straight line from DC to the Rebel capitol of Richmond, just ninety miles south. Beginning in the spring of 1864, Grant and Lee fought a brutal series of battles that filled up northern hospitals and produced over 100,000 Union casualties. However, when the smoke cleared in April 1865, Grant had overpowered and outlasted Lee. The two met at a house in a town called Appomattox Court House, Virginia. Here, Lee surrendered his army to Grant, ending the worst loss of life in American history. Grant was the man who ended the war.

D.Y.K.A.

A GENERAL'S LOVE!

Grant was well-known for his love of cigars. He smoked up to twenty cigars a day. When the war ended, a grateful nation mailed him stogies by the barrelful to thank him for his service to the country.

"BUFFALO BILL" CODY
(1846-1917)
SHOWMAN OF THE WEST

William F. Cody was born on the frontier of Iowa to Canadian parents who opposed slavery. Cody's father was stabbed by a member of a proslavery mob and eventually died. At the age of eleven, Cody went to work as a mounted messenger and a scout. He soon became very skilled at horse wrangling, fighting Indians, and hunting.

He joined the army during the Civil War at the age of seventeen. After the war, he worked again as a civilian scout (someone who is not a soldier) for the US Army in Kansas. He then took a job as a buffalo hunter for the Union Pacific Railroad to provide food for the construction crews. He killed over 4,000 buffalo in two years and was given the nickname "Buffalo Bill."

He was soon in demand as an expert scout and **marksman**. He knew Indian ways and displayed great courage and endurance. The US Army often used him to help wipe out any Native Americans who opposed white settlement. He was even awarded the Medal of Honor in 1872.

His adventures were soon known by the world through newspapers and books. The books described him as a hard-riding, fast-shooting, western folk hero. Cody was offered a part in a dramatized play about the Wild West called *The Scouts of the Prairie* with other famous Western people like "Wild Bill" Hickok.

After ten years of doing the show, Cody created his own show, *Buffalo Bill's Wild West Show*, in 1883 that toured all over the United States and Europe, including a show for Queen Victoria in England. The show featured the famous **markswoman** Annie Oakley and the legendary Chief Sitting Bull with twenty of his braves. The show gave crowds a safe taste of the West and made Cody one of the most well-known celebrities in the world. At his death in 1917, tributes were made by King Edward of England, Kaiser Wilhelm of Germany, and President Woodrow Wilson, to name a few.

D.Y.K.A.

CODY, WYOMING!
The town of Cody, Wyoming, and the east entrance to Yellowstone National Park are part of the legacy of Buffalo Bill Cody. He scouted the area and lobbied the federal government to allow the new entrance. He even paid for the construction of the east entrance out of his own pocket. He also helped create the town of Cody, launched its first newspaper, built hotels, and got the railroad to come. That's a legend in action!

BRIGHAM YOUNG
(1801-1877)
COLONIZER OF THE WEST

Born in Vermont in 1801, Brigham Young was apprenticed as a carpenter and a glazier (glass worker) at the age of fourteen. Years later, he became a follower of the Mormon **prophet** Joseph Smith. When Smith was killed by an armed mob in 1844, Young was soon established as the new leader of the church. In this role, he had a major influence in the settlement of the West.

Under Young's leadership, thousands of Mormons (members of the Church of Jesus Christ of Latter Day Saints) headed west on a modern **exodus** to the promised land of Utah, where they could live in peace. They even blazed a path on the opposite side of the river from the Oregon Trail to avoid any further trouble. When they first arrived in the Salt Lake Valley, Young declared, "This is the right place." Yet Brother Brigham didn't stop there. He sent settlers to colonize the rest of Utah and areas of Idaho, Wyoming, Nevada, Arizona, California, southern Colorado, and northern Mexico. Some of these settlements we know today as San Bernardino, California; Las Vegas, Nevada; and Mesa, Arizona.

Young was the first **governor** of the Utah Territory, which included Nevada, western Colorado, and part of Wyoming. He led the people (Mormon and non-Mormon) to lay the foundations of modern civilization in the West, including roads and bridges, forts, **irrigation** projects, government (he organized the first legislature and the first postal service), the arts (he directed the creation of the Mormon Tabernacle Choir), and education. In fact, he started rival schools, first organizing what is now the University of Utah and later creating Brigham Young Academy, which became Brigham Young University.

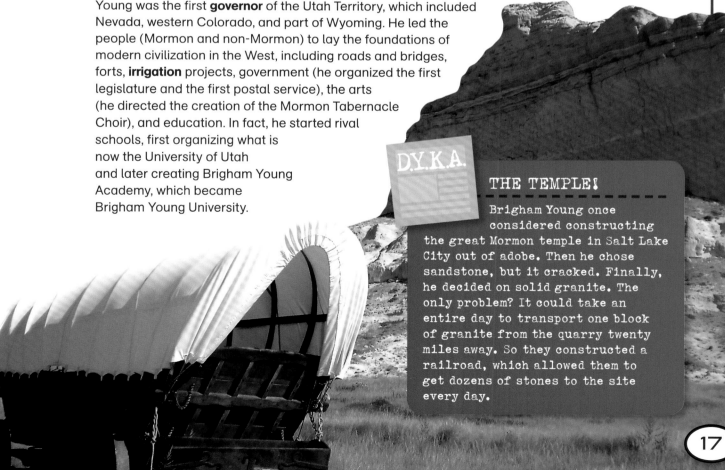

D.Y.K.A.

THE TEMPLE!
Brigham Young once considered constructing the great Mormon temple in Salt Lake City out of adobe. Then he chose sandstone, but it cracked. Finally, he decided on solid granite. The only problem? It could take an entire day to transport one block of granite from the quarry twenty miles away. So they constructed a railroad, which allowed them to get dozens of stones to the site every day.

MARK TWAIN
(1835-1910)
THE FATHER OF AMERICAN LITERATURE

Storytelling was always in Samuel Clemens' blood. While his father was an unsmiling, strict man, his mother would often spin entertaining tales for the children. Perhaps she's the reason why Clemens (later known as Mark Twain) would one day be called the father of American literature by several major authors including Ernest Hemmingway, William Faulkner, and playwright Eugene O'Neil.

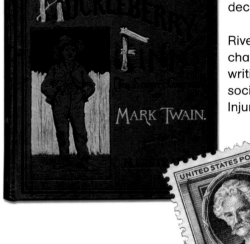

Growing up in the river port of Hannibal, Missouri, in the mid-1800s forever influenced Twain's life and writings. However, poverty also influenced much of Twain's early life due to his father's death in 1847. Many of his choices were an attempt to find riches and respect, as well as adventure. He became a riverboat captain at age twenty-one, which at the time was a very prestigious and well-paid job. Unfortunately, he was forced to quit when the Civil War broke out. Twain then left Missouri to prospect for gold in Nevada and California. He never found the gold, but found a job writing for a newspaper. He had written for his brother, Orion, in Hannibal, and soon took to writing like a fish takes to water. It was then he decided to call himself Mark Twain, a riverboat term for twelve feet of water.

Riverboats and the wide variety of characters they attracted soon filled his writing. Some of his characters hinted at social problems, such as the murderous Injun Joe and Jim, an escaped slave. More than anything, though, his books painted an adventurous picture of what life was like for young boys like Tom Sawyer or Huck Finn who lived on the mighty Mississippi River. His common man attitude, humor, and wit were felt on every page. And his truthful take on American life became a national treasure.

D'où viens-tu? me demanda l'un d'eux.

D.Y.K.A.

A DEATHLY PROPHECY!

Mark Twain was born in 1835, when **Halley's Comet** was in the sky, and he predicted he would die when the comet returned. He was right; he passed away upon the comet's return in 1910.

Edgar Allan Poe
(1809-1849)
American Gothic

Edgar Allan Poe was born to a family of actors in 1809. Death entered the picture early when his mother died when he was only two years old. He was taken to a childless friend, John Allan, whose wife raised him as her own. Poe was sent to England and Scotland for his early school years. He then went to study at the University of Virginia, but he gambled away his money. He moved to Boston, Massachusetts, where he began writing and publishing poetry.

Like many poets, he made no money in the effort. He soon became so poor he joined the military using a false name. When Allan, his foster father, found out, he paid money to have him released and got him into the US Military Academy at West Point. But Poe had no patience for the military. His writing called to him.

Poe moved to Baltimore, Maryland, and published more poetry. He began taking a string of jobs as a newspaper writer and editor. He continued to publish more poetry and some stories such as "The Fall of the House of Usher." He also is credited with starting the detective genre with his story, "The Murders of the Rue Morgue." A short time later, he wrote his most famous poem, "The Raven." It told the tale of a sad and mournful man who wishes he could bring back his beloved Lenore. The poem represented the sadness Poe often felt in his life. "The Raven" was a big hit and made Poe a very famous writer.

Though he was a literary artist, he did not depend on artistic impulses alone to write his stories or poems. He treated his writing as work, outlining and planning it. In fact, French poets Charles Baudelaire and Stéphane Mallarmé praised his methods, calling him a master poet and writer. Most of all, he is known for his dark imagination and the beauty of his haunting stories of horror. Perhaps he spent too much time thinking about death and other mysteries. He was found dead on the streets of Baltimore, Maryland, just after his fortieth birthday, wearing clothes that were not his own. No one knows for sure how he died, but his words will be with us evermore.

D.Y.K.A.

THE PARROT!

Poe once considered using a parrot as the bird in his famous poem, "The Raven." But a colorful parrot did not fit the sad tone of his poem, so he chose a raven since it was a symbol of **superstition** and bad omens. Raven want a cracker?!

19

GERONIMO
(1829-1909)
THE LAST APACHE

In 1829, Geronimo was born into the Apache Indian tribe, who lived in Texas, New Mexico, Arizona, and northern Mexico. As Mexican and American settlers moved into the area during the 1800s, they found the Apache to be unwilling to let go of the land. Regular fighting took place as a result, and because Geronimo was a young warrior, he was part of the violence. But in 1858, his life changed forever when Mexican soldiers killed his wife and their three children. This fueled a hatred for settlers that Geronimo held onto for the rest of his life.

A half-century of warfare led to the gradual reduction of the Apache tribe, and by 1876, the

US government ordered that all Apache must move to the dismal San Carlos **Reservation** in southern Arizona. Like many proud Indian warriors, Geronimo had no interest in reservation life, and he and many other Apache held out as the US Army attempted to round up his people.

Though Geronimo was not a chief, Native Americans viewed him as a leader due to his courage in battle. White settlers knew Geronimo well, calling him "the worst Indian who ever lived." Because he was so feared, the US government sent 5,000 troops to track him down and capture him, dead or alive.

Finally, in 1886, Geronimo found himself hopelessly surrounded and outnumbered, and he realized he could fight no more. A negotiator told him that if he surrendered, he would be sent to Florida for a short time, and then would be allowed to return to his home in Arizona. However, once captured, he remained a prisoner for the rest of his days. He was held in camps in Florida and Oklahoma, and was never allowed to return to Arizona.

For the American public, fear of Geronimo turned to fascination. Geronimo sold souvenirs of himself, appeared in fairs, and even rode in Teddy Roosevelt's 1905 inaugural parade. But sadly, in February 1909, he was thrown from his horse and laid on the cold ground all night until a friend found him. Pneumonia set in and he died just days later. Before dying, he confided that he regretted ever allowing soldiers to take him alive.

D.Y.K.A.

GRAVE ROBBERS!

It is rumored that some Yale University students visited Geronimo's gravesite in Oklahoma and stole his skull during World War I. The rumor holds that the students dug up Geronimo in 1918 and brought his skull and silver bridle back to a secret location on their campus. In 1986, a lawyer representing students at Yale denied that the skull was on the campus. Even so, in 2009, descendants of Geronimo sued to get his skull back, but they had no success in their effort.

CRAZY HORSE
(1840-1877)
THE GREAT SIOUX

Crazy Horse was a chief of the Sioux Indians, a massive group of tribes that dominated the northern Great Plains. The California Gold Rush of 1849 and the Colorado Gold Rush of 1859 brought white settlers into Sioux territory, and this led to frequent gun battles between US soldiers and Sioux warriors. During this time, Crazy Horse became well-known due to his leadership role in the 1866 Fetterman **Massacre**. This was an episode in which Crazy Horse tricked eighty-one US soldiers into leaving the safety of their fort to chase after a small band of Indians. Crazy Horse led 2,000 Arapaho, Cheyenne, and Sioux warriors in an ambush of the US soldiers, killing them all.

Conflict between the Sioux nation and the US government seemed to be resolved in 1868, when the **Treaty** of Fort Laramie gave the Sioux a massive reservation in and around current-day South Dakota. However, gold was discovered on the reservation in an area called the Black Hills in 1874, so the US government offered the Sioux six million dollars for the land that had gold. The Sioux refused, so US troops forced the Indians off the land. This led to the Battle of Little Big Horn (June 1876), one of the most amazing battles in US history. Here, Crazy Horse and fellow Sioux chief Sitting Bull killed over 260 US soldiers, including their leader, George Custer. Even so, the Sioux eventually lost the war and had to give up their rights to the Black Hills.

In 1877, just one year after his magnificent victory at Little Big Horn, Crazy Horse turned himself in to US authorities. He agreed to live peacefully on a reservation. However, four months after moving onto the reservation, US authorities attempted to place Crazy Horse under arrest. A scuffle took place, and a soldier used a bayonet to stab the Indian chief. Crazy Horse died that night.

D.Y.K.A.

THE WORLD'S LARGEST STATUE!

A statue of Crazy Horse that could one day be among the largest stone statues in the world is currently being carved into the Black Hills of South Dakota. Carving began in 1948 on the Crazy Horse Monument, and in 1998 the head of Crazy Horse was completed. That portion alone is eighty-seven-feet tall, which is much taller than the heads of the US presidents at nearby **Mount Rushmore.**

BENJAMIN FRANKLIN
(1706-1790)
AMERICA'S FOUNDING FATHER

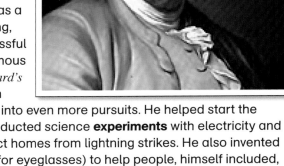

From the time he was a small boy, Benjamin Franklin was coming up with inventions and ideas. He was constantly on the lookout for ways to improve just about everything in life. He even created swim fins as a boy so he could swim faster.

He started out his working career as a printing apprentice, and before long, he was writing and editing a successful newspaper. He also printed his famous book of wit and wisdom, *Poor Richard's Almanack*. This book made Franklin a wealthy man, and he soon dived into even more pursuits. He helped start the University of Pennsylvania. He conducted science **experiments** with electricity and invented the lightning rod to protect homes from lightning strikes. He also invented things like bifocals (a type of lens for eyeglasses) to help people, himself included, see better in their old age. Franklin was the first postmaster and started the first lending library in America, as well as the first fire department in Pennsylvania.

Best of all, Franklin was known as a **diplomat** and a courageous **statesman**. He opposed injustice wherever it occurred and even got England to repeal the hated Stamp Act that unfairly taxed the American colonies. He often represented America in foreign nations like France and Sweden. Of course, he was instrumental in the creation of the Declaration of Independence along with Thomas Jefferson, John Adams, Roger Sherman, and Robert Livingston. During the Revolutionary War, he was also able to convince France to help America. In fact, it was the French ships that helped win the important battle at Yorktown. When the US Constitution was created after the war, Franklin was there to add his voice of wisdom and reason. To this day, Franklin's name and face can be found in cities, in counties, in companies, on navy ships, and even on US stamps and currency.

D.Y.K.A.

BEN FRANKLIN'S KITE!

Benjamin Franklin once flew a kite in a thunderstorm to prove that lightning had an electrical charge. He made sure he was grounded so he wouldn't be electrocuted. Other people tried to duplicate his experiment and didn't understand the need to be grounded. They got quite a shock. Ouch!

THOMAS EDISON
(1847-1931)
THE WIZARD OF MENLO PARK

Thomas Edison was born in 1847 in Milan, Ohio, and started experiments in science and business at an early age. He actually burned down his father's barn in one failed attempt, but Edison never saw his experiments as failures. He once said in his later years, "I have not failed. I've just found 10,000 ways that won't work!" As a boy, he sold candy and newspapers on trains in Michigan as well as selling vegetables on the side. He developed a keen business sense in those early years that would serve him well as an adult.

His next job came when he saved the station agent's three-year-old son from a runaway train. The station agent was so grateful that he trained Edison as a **telegraph** operator. The job didn't last long though. Edison asked for a night shift so he could devote time to his two favorite activities: reading and experimenting. Unfortunately, he spilled sulfuric acid during an experiment one night. The acid leaked down through the floorboards and onto his boss's desk. He was fired the next day, but within two years he had gotten his first **patent**. It was for an electric vote recorder, and it would be the first of over a thousand patents.

In Menlo Park, New Jersey (now renamed Edison, New Jersey), Edison developed what would be known as the first industrial research **laboratory**. Edison knew he needed help to get past the failures and find the solutions, so he employed many others to work with him in the lab. There they created a host of inventions, many of which bear his name. Up until his death in 1931, he was constantly pushing the boundaries of technology and innovation.

Most people are aware of his invention of the first practical electric light bulb and the fact that Edison started General Electric. His accomplishments seemed so magical to the public that they called him the "Wizard of Menlo Park." A few of his other creations (and that of his lab) were the phonograph, the first device to allow you to record and playback music or voice; power systems to power his new light bulb; the kinetograph, the first movie camera; and the kinetoscope, a movie viewer. He truly was a wiz!

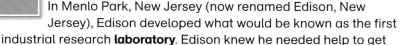

I want to see a Phonograph in every American Home

Thomas A. Edison

The New Edison

Thomas A. Edison's Final Achievement

D.Y.K.A.

EDISON'S AMAZING WAREHOUSE!
Edison wanted his lab to have anything an inventor would need to experiment, so he stocked it with everything imaginable: 8,000 kinds of chemicals, every kind of screw made, every size of needle, every kind of cord or wire, human and animal hair, silk, cocoons, animal hooves, shark's teeth, deer horns, tortoise shells, cork, resin, varnish and oil, ostrich feathers, a peacock's tail, amber, rubber, all ores, and much more!

HELEN KELLER
(1880-1968)
A VOICE OUT OF THE DARKNESS

Helen Keller was an unusually bright child. She was walking and talking by her first birthday. Six months later, she fell ill to an unknown disease and became deaf and blind. As she grew older, though, her frustration with her condition pushed her parents to find a teacher to help young Helen.

Anne Sullivan came to the Keller plantation in Alabama. Once she arrived, she tried to teach Keller sign language for the different objects around her. Keller just got more frustrated, but Sullivan didn't give up. She took Keller to a cottage on the plantation away from the rest of the family. There, Sullivan got Keller to make the connection between the words she was spelling in her hands and the world around her. Sullivan pumped water over Keller's hands as she spelled out the word water in them. Finally, Keller understood and demanded that Sullivan teach her more. That first day, she learned thirty new words in sign language, and that was just the beginning.

Keller attended college with Sullivan as an interpreter. With her help, Keller was able to earn a bachelor's degree—the first for a blind/deaf person. After college, she wrote her own autobiography and lectured around the country and the world. She also helped found the American Civil Liberties Union (ACLU) in 1920. Eventually, her story was made into a movie just before her death. It's a story that continues to inspire millions to overcome their own personal obstacles.

D.Y.K.A.

HELEN KELLER'S FRIENDS!

Helen Keller's story caught the attention of author Mark Twain. They soon became friends, and he introduced her to millionaire Henry Rogers of Standard Oil. He was so impressed with Keller's determination and drive that he agreed to fund her education. Keller would never forget the act and dedicated one of her books to Rogers and his wife.

ANDREW CARNEGIE
(1835-1919)
THE ORIGINAL MAN OF STEEL

Andrew Carnegie was born in Scotland in 1835, and his family moved to America when he was twelve. They settled near Pittsburgh, Pennsylvania, where Andrew worked twelve hours a day in a factory, dipping machine parts into hot oil. This was a terrible job, but it was typical for many children in the time period. The factory owner knew young Andrew was very smart, so he was moved into the factory office. He was promoted many times and eventually found himself working as an assistant to a powerful railroad company executive. The executive liked Andrew and gave him

valuable stock tips, advice about how to make money buying and selling stocks. Andrew followed the advice. By the time he was in his mid-twenties, these stock purchases made Andrew a wealthy man. In 1863, when he was just twenty-seven, he was making $2,400 a year from his railroad salary, but he made an additional $45,000 from his stock market investments.

Carnegie needed places to invest his money. He looked for business opportunities and discovered the steel industry. Steel is a much stronger and lighter form of iron, and it was just coming into use in the mid-1800s. There was a huge demand for the metal, because it was ideal for railroad tracks and skyscrapers. So as America expanded into a superpower, steel would be an essential ingredient. The world's steel was mostly made in Britain at the time, so Carnegie saw a chance to get in early on an industry that was about to really take off. Carnegie traveled to Britain to observe their steel mills in action. He returned home and built a massive steel mill on the south side of Pittsburgh.

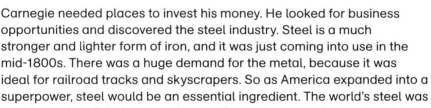

Like John D. Rockefeller, he knew how to cut costs and undersell his opponents. He also pursued **vertical integration**, obtaining coal mines to power his plant, iron ore mines, and railroads to haul his product. By the 1880s, he was America's biggest steel producer, and by the 1890s his company alone was making more steel than all of Britain combined. His presence earned Pittsburgh the nickname "Steel City," which is why its professional football team is called the Pittsburgh Steelers.

By 1901, Carnegie was ready to get out of the business. He sold his company for 492 million dollars in a deal arranged by the famous banker J.P. Morgan. Once the deal was made, Morgan congratulated Carnegie on being the world's richest man. Morgan added other steel mills to Carnegie's to create The United States Steel Corporation. It had a market value of 1.4 billion dollars, making it the nation's first billion dollar company.

D.Y.K.A.

CARNEGIE'S LIBRARIES!

Carnegie is especially remembered for giving his wealth away. He believed it was a disgrace for a wealthy man to die with all his cash. He gave away over 400 million dollars in his lifetime—over ninety percent of what he made. He especially loved to pay for libraries. There are over 2,000 Carnegie libraries in the world today.

CHARLES LINDBERGH
(1902-1974)
PLANE AMAZING

Charles Lindbergh, or "Lucky Lindy" as he was later known, was born in Detroit, Michigan, in 1902, but spent much of his childhood in Minnesota. In fact, his father went on to serve as a US congressman from Minnesota for ten years. His mother was a school teacher, and he often moved from school to school. Through it all, Lindbergh had a growing interest in motorized engines. First it was cars, but then the invention of airplanes captured his imagination. He actually dropped out of his mechanical engineering program at the University of Wisconsin to enter a flying school in Nebraska.

Within a year, Lindbergh bought his first airplane and toured around the country as a daredevil barnstormer performing aerial stunts. Then he trained as an Army Air Service pilot, graduating at the top of his class, despite crashing a plane just eight days before the end of training. It was peacetime though, so Lindbergh found work as an airmail pilot.

Then a French-born hotel owner, Raymond Orteig, offered $25,000 to the first pilot who would make a solo, transatlantic flight from New York to Paris. Many tried and failed (six pilots died in the attempt), but Lindbergh knew it could be done. He got some St. Louis businessmen to support his effort and oversaw the design of the plane. On May 20, 1927, Lindbergh flew into the great unknown. He fought fog, ice, and fatigue and finally landed in Paris thirty-three and a half hours later. Life would never be the same for Lucky Lindy.

Lindbergh was hailed by United States and world leaders for his accomplishment. He was awarded the Medal of Honor and the Distinguished Flying Cross. His plane, the Spirit of St. Louis, was featured on stamps within a month of his feat. He was also asked to consult or advise **aviation** efforts around the globe. Lindbergh was also a huge supporter of scientist Robert Goddard and helped him get the money necessary to develop rocket engines.

Sadly, Lindbergh's baby boy was kidnapped, and he and his wife became very private after the event. In his later years, he continued to advise the US Air Force and even won a Pulitzer Prize in 1954 for his book about his famous flight called, *The Spirit of St. Louis.* Just a few years before his death, he witnessed the launch of *Apollo 11* as they rocketed away to the moon.

D.Y.K.A.

ASKING FOR DIRECTIONS?

On his famous flight to Paris, Lindbergh used every method known to man to navigate: instruments, the stars, guessing, and asking directions. As Lindbergh flew low over the ocean, he spotted some fishing boats. He tried to circle and ask if they would point the way toward land, but they couldn't hear him and so he flew on, finally finding the coast of Ireland on his way to France.

SALLY RIDE
(1951- 2012)
ASTRONAUT

Dr. Sally Kirsten Ride was born in Encino, California, in 1951. From an early age, her parents encouraged her and her sister, Karen, to do their best and study hard in school. Sally showed an early interest in science, so her parents subscribed to *Scientific American* magazine to encourage her to learn more.

Ride also found she had talent for sports, particularly tennis. She was very good and almost became a professional tennis player. She even left college to try to improve her skills. After a few months, she decided to return to college. She launched into learning, becoming a doctor in physics.

As she was finishing her degree, NASA put an advertisement in the student newspaper asking for scientists who were interested in becoming part of the space shuttle missions. Ride applied, and out of 8,000 people, she was one of thirty-five people selected! Six were women—the first female astronauts ever selected for the US space program!

Ride trained hard for four years doing physical training and flight training, as well as studying more science, math, meteorology (weather and climate), guidance, navigation, and everything about the shuttle. Finally, in June of 1983, Ride lifted off as part of the crew of the Space Shuttle *Challenger*. Not only was she the first American woman in space, but at thirty-two, she was also the youngest astronaut ever! A little over a year later, she flew on another shuttle mission and was scheduled for a third mission when disaster struck. In 1986, the Space Shuttle *Challenger* blew up just after launch. Ride would help NASA discover the reasons why it exploded, but she would never fly another space mission.

Ride knew she wouldn't be an astronaut forever and had already decided to become a professor. She taught physics at the University of California at San Diego and was the director of the California Space Institute. She also wrote books for elementary and middle school kids to encourage them (especially girls) to study science and reach for the stars, just like she did!

D.Y.K.A.

SALLY'S TENNIS DAYS!

Sally Ride almost became a professional tennis player instead of an astronaut and professor. She was ranked eighteenth on the national junior tennis circuit and had a promising future. Even tennis legend Billy Jean King felt she had the talent to be a pro tennis player. Good thing she decided to go back to college, or someone else might have been the first American woman in space!

OPRAH WINFREY
(1954-)
VOICE OF THE PEOPLE

Oprah Winfrey was born in rural Kosciusko, Mississippi, to a teenage mother. She was so poor she wore dresses made of potato sacks. Her grandmother taught her to read before she was three, and she could recite Bible verses at an early age. She was also known for playing games where she interviewed her corncob doll and the crows that perched on the fence near her home.

Then she moved to an inner-city neighborhood with her mother in Milwaukee, Wisconsin. It was a dark time for Winfrey. She was abused by relatives, but no one believed her. She made some poor choices that almost trapped her in a life of poverty. Finally, she moved to Nashville, Tennessee, to live with her father, where she began to find her voice.

In high school, Winfrey won second place in a national speech contest! She started doing the news part-time on a local radio station. After college, she worked as a news anchor on a TV station in Nashville, then Baltimore, Maryland, and finally Chicago, Illinois, where she was the host of *AM Chicago*. Within a few months, her ratings (how many people watch a TV show) went from last to first place! So they changed the name of the show to *The Oprah Winfrey Show* and started broadcasting nationally in 1986.

Winfrey's show was the number one talk show in America from that time until its final show in May of 2011. It appealed to so many people because she was genuine and likable, often shedding tears when told heartfelt stories by her guests. She enabled them to open up and reveal things they never told any other talk show host. She was able to get interviews no other show could get, like Michael Jackson at the height of his fame in 1993 (the most watched interview in the history of television)! She even won an Academy Award nomination for her role in filmmaker Steven Spielberg's *The Color Purple*. Soon everyone followed Winfrey's every move, and she created a media brand that made her one of the wealthiest people on the planet. Money wasn't her only goal though. She wanted social change. Her shows often prompted people to read books and consider other points of view and brought a variety of topics to national attention. Today, Winfrey continues to be an inspiration to America and the world!

D.Y.K.A.

OPRAH'S NAME!

Though she is known around the world as Oprah Winfrey, she was actually named after Orpah—a Biblical character in the Book of Ruth. So how did she become Oprah? Her family and friends couldn't pronounce the unusual name and just called her Oprah. The name stuck!

WALT DISNEY
(1901-1966)
SUPREME IMAGINEER

From his days as a boy in rural Marceline, Missouri, Walt Disney was a ball of creative energy. From his first brush with art, Disney was hooked. He loved to draw and paint his world. He even painted pictures of farmyard animals on the side of his father's barn in tar! His father was furious, but his mother saw the budding artist and encouraged him whenever she had the opportunity.

As he grew older, Disney continued to draw. He teamed up with fellow artist Ub Iwerks and together they started a company to create animated short films for local businesses. But Disney wasn't much of a businessman and the company failed.

Disney then moved to California and teamed up with his older brother, Roy. Roy provided the financial guidance and business sense Walt lacked. With his brother's support, Walt kept trying. When their Oswald the Lucky Rabbit character was taken from them in a bad business deal, Walt created a new character, Mickey Mouse, with the help of his old friend Ub Iwerks. The Disney brothers never looked back. Mickey brought success to the company and paved the way for *Snow White*, the first animated feature film. Despite gloomy predictions, the film was a huge success! Disney was even awarded one large and seven miniature Oscars for the achievement—one for each dwarf.

Over the years, Disney went on to create a number of animated and live-action films at his studio. Then he took some of his artists and studio craftsman and gave them the task of creating an all-new type of entertainment, Disneyland. He called them imagineers since they used their imagination to engineer a new kind of amusement park for families. Though Disney died eleven years after Disneyland first opened, his legacy is found around the world in theme parks, entertainment, and the hearts of those who dare to dream!

D.Y.K.A.

DADDY'S DAY!

Saturdays were Daddy's Day, when Walt Disney took his daughters to Griffith Park to ride the carousel. While he sat and watched them from a park bench, he wished for a more ideal place where families could share fun together. A few years later, Disneyland was born, and families have enjoyed the magic ever since!

FRANKLIN DELANO ROOSEVELT
(1882-1945)
ARCHITECT OF THE NEW DEAL

Franklin Delano Roosevelt was born in New York in 1882. He was an only child, and his mother showered him with attention, so much so, in fact, that when he went away to Harvard in 1900, she went with him, taking an apartment near his. After college, he entered politics and eventually became the governor of New York in 1929.

In 1921, when he was thirty-nine years old, Roosevelt went for a swim in a lake in Maine while on vacation there. After the swim, he went straight to bed, feeling so tired that he could not even remove his swimsuit. He fell asleep, but later woke with a 104-degree temperature. He had been stricken by **polio**. The polio virus had attacked his spinal cord, and he would be **paralyzed** from the waist down for the rest of his life.

For the next eight years, he worked as hard as he could to beat the disability. He would fight for hours at a time, covered in sweat, to move one leg in front of the other. But his iron will could not overcome the reality of polio. He gave up the struggle in 1929, when he became governor of New York. His legs grew feeble and late in his life, they were withered and weak, although his upper body remained robust.

In 1929, the New York Stock Exchange crashed. Nearly overnight, billions of dollars in stocks simply disappeared, one third of working Americans lost their jobs, and America plunged into the Great Depression. With the nation's economy in terrible trouble, Roosevelt was elected president in 1932. Roosevelt felt that the government needed to actively work to create jobs and prime the pump of the economy to get it started again. He called his program the New Deal, and he created thousands of jobs in his effort to get Americans back to work. These newly created government programs put men to work building dams, roads, post offices, and schools. Swamps were drained, trees were planted, and even artists were paid to create art that depicted the events of the era.

Roosevelt was re-elected in 1936, and then in 1940, something that had never happened took place; the president was elected for a third term. Tradition held that presidents only serve two terms, but no law required such a limit. But World War II had broken out in Europe, and Americans, fearing the war would soon involve them, wanted proven leadership in the White House. Roosevelt's leadership during the war was so strong that in 1944, the **unprecedented** happened again—Roosevelt was elected a fourth time. Two months into his fourth term, and just four months before the war ended, Roosevelt died. A stunned nation mourned the loss of the man who had led the country through two of the most serious crises of its history.

D.Y.K.A.

ROOSEVELT'S SECRET!
- -
Because of polio, Roosevelt could not walk and had to use a wheelchair. However, he did not want Americans to know this, so he worked hard to keep this fact a secret. He did not allow photographs to be taken of him in the wheelchair, and very few Americans knew that their four-term president was paralyzed.

RONALD REAGAN
(1911-2004)
THE GREAT COMMUNICATOR

Ronald Reagan was born in 1911 in Tampico, Illinois. In college, he was the kind of person who seemed to be good at everything. He played football, acted in plays, was president of the student body, and was captain of the swim team. In 1937, Reagan went to Hollywood to audition for a job as an actor. He was so impressive that Warner Brothers signed him to a seven-year contract. He immediately went to work, starring in his first film, *Love is on the Air*. He became a major movie star and eventually appeared in over fifty films. However, in 1942, he was called into active army duty for World War II.

After the war, Reagan became interested in politics. In 1964, he gave a speech supporting Republican presidential candidate Barry Goldwater. The speech was so electrifying, people realized Reagan would be an excellent political candidate himself. As a result, he ran for governor of California in 1966 and won. During his eight years as governor of California, Reagan established himself as a major Republican leader. He worked to cut government spending and decrease the role of government in the everyday lives of Californians.

In 1980, Reagan was elected president. At the time of his election, America faced many difficult challenges. The standoff between the United States and the **Soviet Union**, known as the **Cold War**, was in its fifth decade. Both nations were spending billions of dollars on weapons and defense in order to keep up with each other. Unemployment was near ten percent, and **inflation** was choking the American economy. Reagan provided the bold leadership the nation desperately needed. Because of his ability to make great speeches, he was often called the great communicator. His plan for the economy called for lower **taxes** and lower government spending to free up cash so Americans could invest and spend as they needed. This approach worked! Jobs were created and inflation came down.

Reagan also helped bring an end to the Cold War with the Soviets using his speech-making ability. In 1987, he gave a famous speech in Berlin in which he spoke directly to the leader of the Soviets saying, "Mr. Gorbachev, tear down this wall." The Soviet Union was a **communist** nation where people had very few rights. The Berlin Wall was part of a dividing line between free and communist countries called the Iron Curtain. By asking the Soviet leader to tear down the wall, Reagan was urging the Soviets to grant freedom to the many communist nations they controlled. In 1989, the wall began to come down, and by 1991 the Soviet Union became the Russian Federation, or Russia.

By the time Reagan left office, he had restored American economic power and re-established American military confidence around the world. His policies created thousands of jobs and made America, once again, a proud, patriotic, and prosperous nation.

D.Y.K.A.

THE GREAT COMMENTATOR!

After graduating from college, Reagan got a job as a sports radio announcer in Iowa. He did play-by-play broadcasts of University of Iowa football games and announced Chicago Cubs games.

A Song in Their Hearts

Louis Armstrong
(1901-1971)
"Satchmo"

Louis Armstrong was born in New Orleans, Louisiana, surrounded by the sounds of jazz music. He marveled at the popular musicians and sang with his friends on the streets for nickels and pennies. Then on New Year's Eve of 1913, he was arrested for firing a gun in the air in celebration. He was sentenced to the Colored Waifs Home, where he was taught to play the **cornet**. He was imitating the leading jazz players, including King Oliver.

Oliver was so impressed with Armstrong that he invited him to join his band in Chicago. Armstrong married the band's pianist, Lil Hardin, who encouraged Armstrong to go solo. He soon played with big orchestras and created his famous Armstrong Hot Five and Hot Seven recordings during the mid-1920s.

Armstrong then switched to the trumpet, and no one could match his technique, his sense of harmony, or his gift for melody. His musical energy flowed through his horn, and the recordings were milestones in jazz music. Armstrong moved to New York and began using his gift for **improvisation** with more popular tunes from **composers** like Fats Waller, Duke Ellington, Hoagy Carmichael, and Irving Berlin. He also began using his gravelly voice to sing and perform vocal improvisations called scat singing, a style he helped invent.

Armstrong went on to appear in movies and toured almost constantly, growing jazz music wherever he went. He was an ambassador of jazz music, and his efforts turned jazz music from a passing fad to a real art form.

D.Y.K.A.

SATCHELMOUTH!

Louis Armstrong is often known by his nickname, "Satchmo," which was short for "Satchelmouth." As he played, his cheeks would inflate like a balloon, looking much like a bag or satchel. A London magazine editor used the shorter version in 1932, and Armstrong liked it so much he used it for an album title.

BIGGEST EVENT OF THE SEASON! Week of July 21-27
OUR OWN
Louis Armstrong
World-Famous Trumpet Soloist And His Orchestra
AT THE
GOLDEN DRAGON
SUNDAY MATINEE - 4 to 8 P.M.
Admission 75c., tax 12c., total 87c.
SUNDAY NIGHT 10 P.M. to 3 A.M.
Admission $1.00, tax 15c., total $1.15
MONDAY NIGHT, 10 P.M. to 3 A.M.
Admission $1.00, tax 15c total $1.15
Balance of Weekly Schedule
FREE! - Tuesday and Thursday - FREE!
RHAPSODIANS ORCHESTRA
SATURDAY NIGHT
Four Pals

ELVIS PRESLEY
(1935-1977)
THE KING

Elvis Aaron Presley was born in a humble home in Tupelo, Mississippi, during the Great Depression. His parents moved a lot, but they attended church regularly where gospel music became a major influence. Presley won a talent show at the age of ten, and a year after graduating from high school, he recorded his first song. A year after that, Presley had his first number one hit with "Heartbreak Hotel," and his first number one album, *Elvis Presley*, as well as a movie deal with Paramount Pictures. Soon Presley seemed to be everywhere— at the movies, on the radio, and on a host of television programs. But

like any American boy of his age, he was **drafted** into military service, where he spent a year and a half in Germany. Upon completion of his service in the army, Presley picked up where he left off and continued to act in movies such as *Blue Hawaii* (1961) and *Viva Las Vegas* (1964).

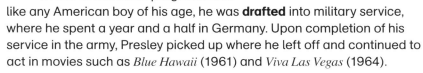

In 1968, when his popularity seemed to be shrinking, Presley performed in his first television special and showed the world what a musical force he was. Around the same time, he also got married and had a baby girl. Things seemed to be looking up for the king of rock and roll!

Sadly, within a few short years, his marriage fell apart. Presley was also battling an addiction to prescription drugs and a weight problem. Still he remained popular with the public until his death from heart failure in 1977 at his home, Graceland, in Memphis, Tennessee. Fans still flock to Graceland today, which is now a museum, and his eighteen number one hit songs are classics that still have people a rockin' and a rollin'!

D.Y.K.A.

TWIN KINGS!

Believe it or not, Elvis Presley was actually an identical twin. His brother, Jesse, was born thirty-five minutes before Elvis, but he was stillborn (died before birth). Would there have been two kings of rock and roll? We'll never know.

CIVIL PIONEERS

SUSAN B. ANTHONY
(1820-1906)
CRUSADER FOR WOMEN'S RIGHTS

Susan B. Anthony was born in Massachusetts to a Quaker family, who had many strong beliefs. They opposed slavery and supported the temperance movement. (The temperance movement was a group of people who wanted to ban the drinking of alcohol.)

Like her parents, Anthony also became involved in the anti-slavery and temperance movements. One day in 1852, Anthony was not allowed to speak at a temperance conference because she was a woman. So she banded together with her friend Elizabeth Cady Stanton and together they began to fight for women's rights, especially the right to vote.

In 1868, she created a weekly newspaper called *The Revolution* to make people aware of women's issues. She also joined with Stanton and founded the National Woman's **Suffrage** Association. She wanted to fight for the right to vote in court, so she attempted to vote for the president in 1872. She was arrested, but there was no court case, only a fine.

That didn't stop her though. She kept giving lectures and speeches on women's rights and even published a series of books on the history of women's rights. Though she died in 1906, other women continued to fight for the cause. Finally, in 1920, Anthony's work paid off and the Nineteenth Amendment to the Constitution passed. Women were allowed to vote!

D.Y.K.A.

SUSAN'S CHILDHOOD!

As a child, Susan B. Anthony rarely played with toys. Her father actually forbade toys or amusements in the house, so the children could focus on more spiritual matters.

Dr. Martin Luther King Jr.
(1929-1968)
American Dreamer

Martin Luther King Jr. was born in 1929 in Atlanta, Georgia. After graduating from college, he went to a **seminary** to learn to become a pastor. After receiving a PhD from a Boston seminary in 1954, he became the pastor of Dexter Avenue Baptist Church in Montgomery, Alabama. His $4,200 salary made him the highest paid African-American pastor in the city. Nineteen months after starting the job, King's life was changed forever when a forty-three-year-old African-American seamstress named Rosa Parks was arrested in Montgomery. She had broken a city law by refusing to give up her bus seat to a white man. To protest this injustice, Dr. King organized a year-long **boycott** of city buses. Thanks to his leadership, the boycott was successful, and the American Civil Rights Movement had begun.

As a result of his leadership in the Montgomery Bus Boycott, Dr. King became the leader of the Civil Rights Movement. For the next twelve years, Dr. King traveled the nation working to change America into a place where black people could enjoy the same basic privileges as white people. As he worked for change, King used his pulpit to preach a message of love and nonviolent protest. He urged his followers to conduct themselves with dignity and to meet hatred with love. In the 1960s, American cities exploded with anger and violence as African-Americans demanded justice, and white groups like the Ku Klux Klan worked to keep things the way they had been. King was arrested over thirty times during this period, as many southern leaders did not welcome the change he promoted.

In 1968, the garbage workers of Memphis went on strike. Dr. King flew there to lead a peaceful march through the city on behalf of the workers. In the evening of April 4, as King stood on the balcony outside his hotel room, he was struck in the head by a rifle bullet. Escaped convict James Earl Ray took the shot from a bathroom window of a nearby boarding house. The bullet struck King in the head, severing an artery in his neck. Within seconds, he was dead. Americans reacted in outrage and despair. Rioting broke out in over 150 cities, and over fifty people died in the violence that night. The greatest light of the 1960s had been tragically snuffed out.

D.Y.K.A.

DR. KING'S SCHOOL DAYS!

King was a very intelligent child. By the time he was five years old, he talked as if he were an adult. When he was fifteen years old, his teachers felt he had learned all that high school had to offer, so he enrolled in college. He graduated from college when he was only nineteen.

ALVIN C. YORK
(1887-1964)
THE SHOOTER

Alvin C. York was born in 1887 and grew up on a farm in Tennessee. He learned how to shoot a rifle from his father, and since the family hunted in order to eat, being good at shooting was important. York was particularly skilled at shooting wild turkeys. He would attend country turkey shoots, where he would win the contests by shooting a turkey through the head.

When America entered World War I in 1917, four million young men were drafted into the army, and York was one of them. He asked to be excused from duty because he didn't think it was right to kill people, even in war.

However, the army required him to serve anyway. Once he was in the army, his company commander was able to explain to York that sometimes wars have to be fought in order to stop evil rulers from taking the lives of innocent people. Once York understood what World War I was about, he was ready to do his duty.

York and his unit arrived in France on the Western Front in the spring of 1918. He finally saw his first real action in October in the Battle of the Argonne Forrest. At this time, York was a corporal, a low rank in the army.

During the battle, on October 8, York's company was attempting to advance through a valley in order to capture a railroad line. The valley was ringed with German artillery and machine gun nests, and the American soldiers were pinned down under a withering fire. York's lieutenant selected seventeen men to back out of the valley and go around the left side of the battlefield in order to get behind the enemy. As York and the other men hiked through the forest, they entered a clearing where about thirty Germans were sitting down eating breakfast. The Germans put their hands up to surrender.

As the American troops began to disarm this large group of prisoners, Germans in the hills above yelled to the prisoners to hit the ground and then opened fire from machine gun nests. Most of the seventeen Americans were killed or wounded immediately, but York was not hit. Using his rifle, York began to shoot the German gunners as they raised their heads to see him. He did this in the same way he used to shoot turkeys as a boy back in Tennessee. York killed fifteen Germans. Next, seven Germans charged straight at York, running downhill toward him. York had his Colt pistol dangling from his finger and now began to use it. He shot each of the charging Germans, taking out the one in the rear first, and then working forward, so that none of the Germans knew that his comrades were going down. This, too, was a turkey shooting technique.

After seeing such a display of bravery and marksmanship, now over 100 overwhelmed Germans in the area surrendered to York. As he marched these prisoners out of the woods, more Germans joined the group. When he returned to the safety of the American lines, he had 132 prisoners with him. York was awarded the Medal of Honor for his bravery in battle that day.

D.Y.K.A.

THE PERFECT SHOT!

After York turned in his 132 German prisoners, he was asked how many times he had fired his weapons. He reported that he had shot twenty-eight bullets that day. The next day, the site of his heroics was inspected, and twenty-eight dead Germans were found.

AUDIE MURPHY
(1925-1971)
AMERICAN HERO

Because he was the most highly-decorated American soldier of World War II, Audie Murphy was a very special person. But in fact, he was always a very special person. As a young boy, he and his nine brothers and sisters found themselves without a father, so Murphy dropped out of school in the fifth grade to get a job to help support the family. Later, when the Japanese bombed Pearl Harbor in 1941, he was only sixteen, but desperately wanted to go fight for his country. The army required enlistees to be eighteen, so his sister altered his birth certificate. It worked! Just after his seventeenth birthday, the US Army enlisted him in the infantry.

Murphy first saw action in Sicily and Italy in 1943 and 1944 and distinguished himself as an outstanding soldier. He received multiple promotions and medals due to his bravery in combat. However, the bravery he showed on a battlefield in France in 1945 set him apart forever. Outnumbered, Murphy ordered his men to fall back into the woods, while he slowed the Germans with covering fire. He emptied his rifle, then as he prepared to withdraw, he spotted a burning American tank destroyer with a .50 caliber machine gun on it. Ignoring the danger, he jumped on the vehicle and turned its large machine gun against the Germans. Wounded and bleeding, Murphy finally jumped off of the tank destroyer moments before it exploded. His actions stopped a German tank unit and saved the lives of his entire unit.

For his actions that day in France, Murphy won the Medal of Honor, America's highest military award. Murphy showed similar valor on other occasions, and by the time the war ended, he had collected thirty-three awards and decorations in all. These included two Bronze Stars, two Silver Stars, the Distinguished Service Cross, and three Purple Hearts. No other American won so many honors during the war.

After the war, Murphy became a Hollywood film star, appearing in over forty films. His most successful film was called *To Hell and Back*, and it was the true story of his actions in World War II. He played himself.

Sadly, he died in 1971 when his private plane crashed in Virginia. He is buried at Arlington National Cemetery near Washington, DC, and his grave is the second most visited in the cemetery, after John F. Kennedy's.

D.Y.K.A.

TANK KILLER!
Murphy is credited with killing at least 250 Germans during World War II, and destroying six tanks.

THEODORE ROOSEVELT
(1858-1919)
THE ROUGH RIDER

Theodore Roosevelt is probably the most fascinating of all American presidents. Taking office in 1901 after the shooting death of William McKinley, he was the youngest US president ever at age forty-two. He was a speed-reader, going through a book each day. He wrote over twenty books himself, and he also wrote over 150,000 letters. Once, in Milwaukee, he was shot in the chest, but insisted on giving his planned speech before going to the hospital. He also personally led men called the Rough Riders in battle during the Spanish-American War. His is the only modern face among the four presidents on Mount Rushmore.

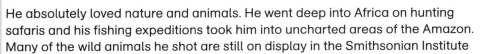

He absolutely loved nature and animals. He went deep into Africa on hunting safaris and his fishing expeditions took him into uncharted areas of the Amazon. Many of the wild animals he shot are still on display in the Smithsonian Institute today. And he, more than any other president, is responsible for the creation of America's beautiful national parks and wildlife preserves. He started the National Park Service and set aside forty million acres of land that will be forever preserved as a natural habitat for plants and animals.

Roosevelt fell in love with the study of animals when he was just a child. This interest began when he was seven and he saw a dead seal displayed at a dock in New York City. It had been killed in the harbor, and he came to see it every day. He bought a pocket ruler and measured the seal's dimensions. After begging for it, he was finally given the animal's skull, which he preserved in his collection.

Theodore Roosevelt came from a fabulously wealthy family. For example, when he was a student at Harvard, the university's president made a salary of $5,000 a year, but Teddy's annual allowance was $8,000. But even though he was wealthy, Teddy cared deeply about helping people in need. As a politician, he was known as a **Progressive**, meaning he worked to make life better for poor and underprivileged Americans. He worked hard to get young children out of factories and into schools, to help immigrants get jobs, and to improve living conditions in the overcrowded **slums** of American cities.

D.Y.K.A.

A VERY CUDDLY BEAR!

Even though Roosevelt loved to hunt animals, he did not shoot everything he saw. Once while hunting in Mississippi in 1902, he refused to shoot a bear that had been tied to a tree by scouts. This story captured the imagination of Americans and led to the creation of a brand new toy, the Teddy Bear.

John F. Kennedy
(1917-1963)
Young Statesman

John F. Kennedy, or JFK as he was known, was born in Massachusetts in 1917, one of nine children from a prominent Irish American family. He attended Harvard University in Cambridge, Massachusetts, and then joined the navy during World War II.

In 1960, Kennedy ran for president against Richard Nixon, and the election was one of the closest in US history. JFK won by just 112,000 out of more than sixty-eight million votes cast. At age forty-three, Kennedy was the youngest man ever elected president. As he took office, Kennedy called for Americans to "ask not what your country can do for you; ask what you can do for your country." He then called on the nations of the world to "ask not what America can do for you, but what together we can do for the freedom of man."

Though he called on world leaders to seek peace and tolerance, he was often forced to defend America from the growing military build-up by the Soviet Union, which came to be known as the Cold War. In the 1962 Cuban Missile Crisis, JFK used a naval blockade to stop nuclear missiles from being shipped to communist Cuba. Kennedy also announced the United States planned to send a man to the moon before the end of the decade (which happened in 1969). Sadly, Kennedy would never see that goal realized. Two bullets from an assassin's rifle struck him as he toured Dallas in a limousine in 1963. He was rushed to nearby Parkland Memorial Hospital, but doctors declared him dead just minutes after his arrival.

D.Y.K.A.

KENNEDY'S SHIPWRECK!

Seventeen years before being elected president, Kennedy became famous as a hero of World War II. He was the skipper of *Patrol Torpedo Boat 109* (*PT-109*), and in August 1943, a massive Japanese destroyer actually drove through the ship, cutting it in two. Two crewmen died in the wreck, but eleven, including Kennedy, managed to swim to a deserted island. Kennedy's leadership and swimming ability saved the lives of many of his men. Rescued six days later, the story appeared in nearly every newspaper in the country.

MIA HAMM
(1972-)
SOCCER STAR

Mariel Margaret Hamm was born in Selma, Alabama, in 1972. Her mother, a ballet dancer, gave her the nickname "Mia" in honor of her mother's dance mentor, Mia Slavenska. She's been called Mia ever since. Of course, it was a strange nickname for a child born with partial club feet (a condition where the feet are turned inwards). To correct the defect, she wore special shoes. But that didn't slow little Mia down. According to her father, Mia saw someone playing soccer when she was eighteen months old, and she ran over and kicked the ball!

As a child, Hamm learned to play soccer while living in Italy (her father was an US Air Force pilot). It was clear that she had a gift for the game. She went on to play for the US Women's Soccer Team at the age of fifteen. She entered college at seventeen and helped the University of North Carolina win four national championships. Hamm also played on the US World Cup team with Michelle Akers, Brandi Chastain, and Kristine Lilly in 1991. The US Women's Soccer Team won the first FIFA Women's World Cup in 1991, making Hamm (nineteen at the time) the youngest player to ever win the World Cup. The win turbo-charged the growth of soccer in America. Soccer teams and leagues grew like never before.

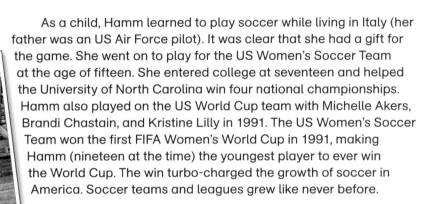

When Hamm and the members of the team played in the 1999 World Cup at the Rose Bowl in California, over 90,000 people attended the game, making it the highest-attended women's sporting event in history to date! To top it off, they won their second World Cup, making them one of the most dominant teams in the sport. Year after year, the team went on to win Olympic Gold Medals (1996, 2004) and made the semi-finals of every FIFA Women's World Cup ever since. Hamm and teammate Michelle Akers were both put on the list of FIFA's 125 greatest living soccer players. They were the only women and the only Americans to make the list. Hamm was also named the FIFA World Player of the Year in 2001 and 2002. Today Hamm enjoys helping people through her Mia Hamm Foundation that studies bone marrow and blood diseases, like the one that killed her brother, Garrett, in 1997. She is also mother to twin girls and likes to encourage kids everywhere to follow their dreams and play soccer!

D.Y.K.A.

MIA'S FOOTBALL CAREER!

Mia Hamm knows how to find a net, but soccer wasn't her only sport growing up. She actually played football in junior high school for Notre Dame Catholic School in Wichita Falls, Texas. Hamm played split end and defensive back for the team.

Michael Jordan
(1963-)
His Airness

Michael Jordan was born in Brooklyn, New York, but moved to Wilmington, on the coast of North Carolina, as a toddler. There his competitive spirit soared while playing football, basketball, and baseball. Soon, basketball became Jordan's focus, earning him a scholarship to the University of North Carolina and honors as a McDonald's All-American.

His first year in college brought even more honors, as he was named the Atlantic Coast Conference (ACC) Freshman of the Year. The next year, in 1982, he made the winning jump shot in the NCAA championship game against Georgetown (led by future pro-star, Patrick Ewing). The win was a major turning point in Jordan's career, and two years later, in 1984, he left school to join the NBA, playing for the Chicago Bulls (though he finished his college degree the next year).

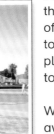

Jordan made an instant splash in the league, earning the Rookie-of-the-Year Award and making his first of fourteen appearances in the All-Star Game. He took the Bulls to their first appearance in the NBA playoffs, but it wasn't until 1991 that he led them to the championship three years in a row!

When his father was killed in a robbery, Jordan stepped away from the court and decided to play baseball for the minor league team Birmingham Barons. The time away seemed to energize Jordan, who returned to the Bulls and helped them win three more championships before retiring again. Of course, the pictures of Jordan sailing through the air and dunking the ball from the foul line live on in the minds of basketball fans everywhere.

D.Y.K.A.
MICHAEL'S GROWTH SPURT!

Michael Jordan tried out for his high school varsity basketball team his sophomore year. He didn't make it. The reason? They thought he was too short to compete (he was five feet eleven inches tall). He proved them wrong with several forty-point games on the junior varsity team, and he grew four inches over the summer. The next year he made varsity.

SANDRA DAY O'CONNOR
(1930-)
SUPREME COURT JUSTICE

Born in El Paso, Texas, Sandra Day O'Connor grew up on an Arizona cattle ranch, but stayed with her grandmother in El Paso for most of her schooling. She attended Stanford University, where she received a degree in economics in 1950, and then attended Stanford's law school.

Though she was a star student in law school, no **law firm** in California would hire her because she was a woman. So she started out in public service as an attorney for San Mateo County, California, and later became the Assistant Attorney General of Arizona. After a few years, she was appointed to the Arizona Legislature by Republican Governor Jack Williams.

She was re-elected for two more terms and became the first female majority leader in a state legislature. Returning to court, O'Connor was elected to the Maricopa County Superior Court in Arizona. Later, Democratic Governor Bruce Babbitt appointed her to the Arizona Court of Appeals. Then in 1981, President Ronald Reagan nominated her for the US Supreme Court. She was confirmed by an unheard-of unanimous, **bipartisan** vote of ninety-nine to zero by the US **Senate**.

Though O'Connor often voted along with other **conservative** justices in key court cases, she was the deciding vote against overturning *Roe v. Wade*, the case that made abortion legal. She always used the law and the US Constitution as guiding documents when it came to cases. But when her husband became ill with Alzheimer's disease, she decided to retire to spend more time with him and her family. In recognition of her achievements, President Barack Obama awarded her the Presidential Medal of Freedom in 2009. She continues to inspire future generations!

D.Y.K.A.

THIS SUPREME COINCIDENCE!

While in law school, Sandra Day O'Connor wrote for the *Stanford Law Review*. She briefly dated the presiding editor-in-chief and future US Supreme Court Chief Justice William Rehnquist.

Barack Obama
(1961-)
Game Changer

Barack Hussein Obama II was born in Hawaii to a mother from the Midwest and a father from Kenya. The couple had fallen in love and married while at the University of Hawaii, but after two years they separated and later divorced. Obama only saw his father once more in 1971. He often wondered what it might have been like if his father had stayed,

and he wrote about it in his bestselling book, *Dreams of My Father*.

His mother later remarried, and they moved to Indonesia for a few years, then back to Hawaii where Obama lived with his grandparents. His college years were spent in California, then New York, where he attended Columbia University and graduated in 1983.

After graduating from Columbia University, Obama spent time in Chicago as a community organizer, helping **low-income residents**. In this role, he realized that in order to help make the change he thought was necessary, he needed to become more familiar with the law. Determined to act, he went to Harvard Law School, where he became the first African-American president of the *Harvard Law Review*.

Five years after graduation, Obama ran for the Illinois State Senate and won. A few years later, in 2004, Obama was elected to the US Senate. He was the third African-American elected to the Senate since the Civil War. His star continued to rise as he ran for president of the United States. When he won the election, he became the first African-American president, forever shattering the race barrier. An electric sense of hope and change filled the nation as Obama took office in 2009, and again when he won re-election in 2012. Obama made a tremendous impact on modern politics and his legacy continues even after his presidency!

D.Y.K.A.

BARRY!

Barack Obama wasn't always called Barack. Growing up he was known as Barry. It wasn't until college that he insisted on being called Barack.

GLOSSARY

Abolitionist – A person who worked to bring an end to (abolish) slavery in America before the Civil War

Aristocrat – A privileged person who inherits their position; a member of the nobility

Aviation – Flying or making aircrafts

Bipartisan – Involving people from two political parties like Democrats and Republicans

Bleeding Kansas – A series of violent events in the mid-1850s in Kansas in which over 200 people died

Boycott – A refusal to buy from or deal with someone or something

Cold War – Period between 1945 and 1991, in which the United States and the Soviet Union fought for control of various countries around the world

Communist – Supporting or based on communism, a totalitarian system where goods and property are shared

Commissioned – Given or assigned a special job, often for payment

Composer – Someone who writes music

Conservative – Supporting small government, low taxes, and tradition

Congress – The House of Representatives and the Senate; the elected, law-making group of people from each state who create national laws

Congresswoman/man – An elected member of the US House of Representatives

Cornet – An instrument similar to a trumpet with a softer, more mellow sound and shorter metal tubing

Diplomat – Someone who represents a country to other countries or governments, often helping them get along with each other

Drafted – Forced by law to join the army, usually during a time of war

Electoral votes – Votes by members of the Electoral College to elect the US president, based on the votes of US citizens and the populations of the states

Exodus – An event in which a lot people leave a place at once

Expedition – A journey, often for exploration or research

Experiment – A scientific test to learn more about something

Governor – The leader of a state or territory

Halley's Comet – A famous comet (an object in space, which orbits the sun and often has a tail) that is visible from Earth about every seventy-five years

House of Representatives – An elected, lawmaking group based on the number of people living in each state, which allows states with more people to have more votes on new laws

Improvisation – Doing something without preparation, often describing performing arts like music or acting

John Brown – A pre-Civil War abolitionist who led a violent raid on the US arsenal at Harper's Ferry, Virginia, in 1859

Inflation – A rise in the prices of consumer goods

Interpreter – Someone who helps people who speak different languages communicate by translating or explaining

Irrigation – A human-made system to water plants

Laboratory – A place where scientific experiments are done

Law firm – A group of lawyers who do business together

Legislature – An elected group of representatives who vote on laws in a republic

Low-income residents – A group of people who make less money than the average salary

Markswoman/man – Someone who is very good at shooting and hitting targets

Massacre – The killing of a large number of people

Mount Rushmore – A massive monument carved into a mountain in South Dakota featuring the faces of Presidents Washington, Jefferson, Lincoln, and Roosevelt

Paralyzed – Unable to move all, or part, of the body

Patent – A law that stops people from copying others' inventions and making money from it without permission

Plantation – A large farm that uses many workers or slaves who often live on the plantation

Polio – A viral disease that results in paralysis, deformity, and muscular weakness

Progressive – A political party focused on moderate political change and government-driven social change

Prophet – Someone who predicts what might happen in the future, often related to religion

Seminary – A special school that teaches people about religion so they can become a priest, pastor, or rabbi

Senate – An elected, lawmaking group made up of two representatives from each state, giving all states an equal vote on new laws

Soviet Union – A group of communist nations led by Russia that existed between 1922 and 1991

Stateswoman/man – An experienced politician or lawmaker, usually respected by others

Suffrage – The right to vote in elections

Reservation – A piece of land governed by and inhabited by American Indians (though not all American Indians live on reservations)

Slum – An area in a city where many people live in poverty

Superstition – A belief or action that is irrational (doesn't make sense), like thinking black cats are bad luck

Taxes – Money that, by law, must be given to the government to pay for expenses such as roads, schools, police, and firefighting

Telegraph – A machine that allowed messages to be sent over long distances using electricity and wires

Treaty – An agreement between two or more groups, often countries

Term – The length of time an elected representative serves

Unalienable – Impossible to be taken away or given to another person

Unprecedented – Having never happened before

Vertical integration – A system in which many businesses within one company work together on the different steps of making a product

INDEX